7/07

D1371427

BABY FOX

Published in Canada by Fitzhenry & Whiteside, 195 Allstate Parkway, Markham, Ontario L3R 4T8
Published in the United States by Fitzhenry & Whiteside, 121 Harvard Avenue, Suite 2, Allston, Massachusetts 02134

10 9 8 7 6 5 4 3 2 1

U.S. Publisher Cataloging-in-Publication Data
Library of Congress Standards
Lang, Aubrey.
Baby fox / text by Aubrey Lang ; photography by Wayne Lynch. -- 1st ed.
[32] p. : col. photos. ; cm.   (Nature babies)
Summary: In northern Alaska a female red fox is busy with her newborn litter, while her mate hunts
for them both. As the pups grow, they venture farther outside the den, begin to play and fight to develop
their survival and hunting skills, and prepare to leave home.
ISBN 1-55041-688-X
ISBN 1-55041-724-X (pbk)
1. Foxes -- Juvenile literature. [1. Foxes.] I. Lynch, Wayne, 1948- . II. Title. III. Series.
599.775   [E]   21   2002   AC CIP

National Library of Canada Cataloguing in Publication Data
Lang, Aubrey
Baby fox

(Nature babies)
ISBN 1-55041-688-X (bound).--ISBN 1-55041-724-X (pbk.)

1. Foxes--Infancy--Juvenile literature. I. Lynch, Wayne
II. Title. III. Series: Lang, Aubrey. Nature babies.

QL737.C22L33 2002   j599.775'139   C2002-900336-9

Design by Wycliffe Smith

BABY FOX

Text by Aubrey Lang
Photography by Wayne Lynch

Fitzhenry & Whiteside

BEFORE YOU BEGIN

Dear Reader,

We love to watch and photograph wild animals. Often they make us laugh; sometimes they make us cry. We wrote this book to share with you some of the exciting stories in the life of a red fox family, which most people will never see. We prefer to photograph animals in nature, not in zoos. And we take care never to harm our animal subjects or to interfere with them in any way.

To photograph the red foxes in this book, we camped on the edge of the Arctic Ocean, near the Alaskan/ Yukon border. In summer, the sun never sets, and we could watch the foxes twenty-four hours a day.

— Aubrey Lang and Wayne Lynch

TABLE OF CONTENTS

It is a sunny winter day in northern Alaska. The snow sparkles and the sky is as blue as it can be. The snowy world seems quiet and empty.

Suddenly a big, bushy, red tail waves above some willow bushes. It is the tail of a female red fox. She is hunting mice hidden under the snow. A different smell, strong and musty, catches her nose. She stops hunting to follow this new smell.

The strange smell is the urine of a male red fox. It is the winter mating season. The young female fox has never had a mate before. She tracks the male, then watches him from a distance.

At first the female is nervous and runs away when the male trots over to meet her. But soon she accepts him as her mate, and they begin to travel together.

The male fox is a handsome dark animal. Because of his color, the male red fox is also known as a cross fox.

The foxes hunt together and look for a den where they can raise a family. They search inside piles of boulders and under the roots of trees. The two foxes are lucky. They find an old den on the side of a hill, and the female cleans it out. Her babies will be born in about two months.

The male hunts for his mate as well as himself, because now the female fox is busy with a newborn litter of pups. The den is damp and chilly, and the mother must stay with the pups to keep them warm.

The male fox is an expert hunter. His large, sensitive ears listen for the faint sounds of mice and lemmings running in their tunnels under the snow.

There are five pups in the new family: three red and two cross-colored. At three weeks, they begin to peek outside the den. But they are shy and clumsy, and they fall over easily. The color of their fur matches the dirt around the den, so it won't be easy for hungry predators to spot them.

The fox pups find the outside world an exciting place to explore. There are twigs to chew and grass to taste. There is rabbit fur to sniff and nibble, and noisy ravens to watch as they soar overhead.

The two female pups are the biggest in the litter, and they wander farther away from the den.

As the baby foxes grow, they need more food. Now both parents must hunt for their hungry family. Although the pups still nurse, their tiny teeth can chew and suck on small pieces of meat.

The pups are full of energy, but their mother is tired from hunting. She falls asleep after licking her pups clean.

In the first month of life, the pups have many fights to decide who will be the boss of the litter. The parents never interfere while the pups bite, chew, and scratch each other. The fighting stops when the pups decide who is number one, two, three, four, and five. Pup number one steals food from all the others and grows the fastest.

After weeks of fighting, the pups are ready to play. They run, leap, chase, and wrestle. They chew on sticks and bones, and play tug-of-war with pieces of old dried skin. These games help the pups develop their hunting skills and grow strong muscles and bones.

Itch and scratch. Itch and scratch. Now the family den is filled with biting fleas, so the pups spend more time napping outside in the sunshine.

When a pup sees an adult return from hunting, the little one races out to meet it. Whoever gets there first gets the meal. If the pup can't swallow it whole, a food fight will follow.

One day, the mother fox leads her pups to a brand new den, one that has no fleas. On the way, one of the pups accidentally wanders near a pair of jaegers nesting on the ground. The crabby jaegers hover above the frightened pup. They swoop down and try to peck the pup on the head to drive her away. But the little one escapes and runs to her mother.

The new family den is beside a large, half-frozen lake where it is windy and cool. The wind keeps the mosquitoes away.

After the long trip, the pups are tired. Once they fall asleep, their mother goes out to hunt. But the nap is a short one. Soon the excited pups are playing and exploring their new home.

A herd of shaggy muskoxen have come down to the lake for a drink. Without their mother to watch out for them, the pups don't see the large, hairy beasts heading toward the den. When the pups finally notice, they bark in alarm. But that doesn't stop the harmless muskoxen, who ignore the noisy pups and keep moving. With a final yelp, all of the young foxes dive into the den.

By early summer, the pups are almost as big as their parents. The young foxes spend long hours waiting for the adults to return with food. While they wait, they eat anything they can find: caterpillars, beetles, bumblebees and berries. At one time, their parents led them on short hunting trips, but now the adults are rarely home.

Hunger finally forces the young foxes to leave the den. It's time for them to hunt on their own and become independent.

DID YOU KNOW?

- An adult female fox is called a vixen; the adult male is called a dog.

- The red fox is one of the most widespread mammals on Earth. It lives in North America, Europe, Asia, northern Africa and Australia. This adaptable fox lives in deserts, forests, mountains, and arctic tundra.

- A pair of foxes lives in a territory where they hunt and raise their pups. They guard their territory against other foxes, and chase them away. The owners mark the boundaries of their territory with squirts of strong-smelling urine.

- The red fox is a hunter and a scavenger. It hunts insects, small rodents, rabbits, hares, grouse and ducks; and it scavenges any dead animal. The fox stores food it doesn't need in scattered locations throughout its territory, and retrieves it later when food is scarce.

- The average litter contains five pups. In territories where there is plenty of food, the pair may raise as many as nine.

- In Alaska and northern Canada, the majority of red foxes are red in color. Some red foxes have black fur, tipped with white; they are called silver foxes. Others have a mixture of black and reddish-brown fur; they are called cross foxes. All three color variations may occur in a single litter.

- Sometimes young female foxes may stay with their parents over the winter and help them raise their next litter of pups. Young male foxes always leave the family territory in the fall and travel long distances in search of a territory of their own.

INDEX

BIOGRAPHIES

When Dr. Wayne Lynch met Aubrey Lang, he was an emergency doctor and she was a pediatric nurse. Five years after they were married, they left their jobs in medicine to work together as writers and wildlife photographers. For more than twenty years they have explored the great wilderness areas of the world — tropical rainforests, remote islands in the Arctic and Antarctic, deserts, mountains, and African grasslands.

Dr. Lynch is a popular guest lecturer and an award-winning science writer.

He is the author of more than a dozen titles for adults and children. He is also a Fellow of the internationally recognized Explorers Club, and an elected Fellow of the prestigious Arctic Institute of North America.

Ms. Lang is the author of nine nature books for children. She loves to share her wildlife experiences with young readers, and has more stories to tell in the Nature Baby Series.

The couple's impressive photo credits include thousands of images published in over two dozen countries.